"WHO DO YC

KOFI KARIKARI

Table of Contents

All scripture quotations are taken from NKJV

For permission requests, please contact Kofi Karikari at +1 208 801 3478.

Email: Kaykofi7@gmail.com

AUDIOBOOK

https://drive.google.com/file/d/1v5B47mAlb7KNn
7S_meuJs9diM2-v5MFs/view?usp=share_link

SCAN QR CODE OR CLICK LINK FOR
AUDIO BOOK

PREFACE

In the Gospel of Matthew (16:13-19), there's a powerful moment where Jesus asks his friends, "Who do you say I am?" This question isn't just about Jesus' identity—it's a question that echoes through time, touching hearts and stirring thoughts.

"Who Do You Say I Am" is a book inspired by this moment. It's an invitation to explore the importance of this question then and now. It's not just a story; it's a chance to think about what Jesus means to each of us.

In this part of the Bible, Jesus and his friends have a conversation that challenges them to think deeply about who Jesus really is. Their answers show different ideas about him, reflecting what people still think today.

This book isn't about giving you one answer. Instead, it's about asking questions that make you think. Who is Jesus to you? What does he mean in your life and in the world?

"Who Do You Say I Am" takes a closer look at this part of the Bible. It explores why this question matters and how it might be important to us today, no matter what we believe.

This journey through these pages mixes ideas about faith, history, and personal stories. It's meant to get you thinking and talking about what Jesus means to you.

So, as you read, consider Jesus' question: Who do you say I am? And maybe, in thinking about this question, you'll discover new things about yourself and your beliefs.

CHAPTER ONE

"WHO DO MEN SAY THAT I AM"

"When Jesus came into the region of Caesarea Philippi, He asked His disciples, saying, "Who do men say that I, the Son of Man, am?"" Matthew 16:13 NKJV

In Matthew 16:13 downwards, Jesus asks his disciples, *"Who do people say that I am?"* The exposé reveals how people knew Jesus in reference to their relationship with Him.

In answering Jesus' question, some of his disciples responded, "People say you're John the Baptist," by this, they had received Jesus Christ as John the Baptist. Others said, "others say you're Elijah" this is to say that other people also received Jesus Christ as the Prophet Elijah. Some also said, "We see you as Jeremiah, one of the Prophets." All these responses make us realize that people have different revelations about Jesus.

What revelation do you have about Jesus?

I have come to notice that one's revelation reflects on the kind of blessing he has.
Your revelation determines your manifestation;
Your revelation determines your progress;
Your revelation determines your discovery; Your revelation determines your position in life.

Likewise, your manifestation as a child of God is based on the revelation you have about Jesus.

Some referred to Him as the Carpenter's son. "When He had come to His own country, He taught them in their synagogue, so that they were astonished and said, "Where did this Man get this wisdom and these mighty works? Is this not the carpenter's son? Is not His mother called Mary?

And His brothers James, Joses, Simon, and Judas?" Matthew 13:54-55 NKJV

Though Jesus was an anointed Pastor, Prophet, Teacher, Evangelist, and Apostle, He was not recognized as such by His people. Often, people relate with you based on the revelation they have about you. They could not accept Him as "The Anointed" because they knew Him as a Carpenter's son. People are limited by what they don't know in life. It is very difficult to receive what you don't value in life. There is a certain amount of revelation people have on what they value. After some few years of Pastoring people, I have noticed how people relate with God based on what they know about Him. This is the reason why it is important to acquire more knowledge. Your knowledge depicts value.

"That I may know Him and the power of His
resurrection, and the fellowship of His sufferings,
being conformed to His death,"
Philippians 3: 10 NKJV

Knowing more gives you power and reveals things.
To be good at something, just learn more about it.
What you know affects how you see and accept
things. What sets apart a successful man from an
unsuccessful one is the knowledge one has over the
other. What do you know? In Christianity, you will
find both rich and poor people together. The poor
may ask, "why am I poor whilst my friends are rich.
Don't we go to the same church? Don't we pray
together?

Don't we give offerings?" The poor might conclude
by saying "God has not been fair to me". Well, I
believe God has been very fair by giving everyone
an equal opportunity to live. What really makes the

difference is revelation. If you want to be rich, successful, healthy, grow spiritually, anointed, you must have a certain level of revelation about Jesus. Revelation is the key secret to obtaining a greater beginning and end. 'In all thy getting, get revelation.'

CHAPTER 2

"WHAT DO YOU SAY I AM?"

"He said to them, "But who do you say that I am?""
Matthew 16: 15 NKJV

Later in the verses, following the disciples' account of who people think Jesus is, he turns to them and asks, *"But who do you say I AM?"*

We recognize that the disciples had known him based on the revelation others had about Him.

"So, they said, "Some say John the Baptist, some Elijah, and others Jeremiah or one of the prophets."" *Matthew 16:14 NKJV*

Mostly, the things we accept are determined by what we hear in life. What we hear people say, or the report people give about someone, influences our reception. Your knowledge about Christ can be influenced by what people are saying about Him. It is prudent that we know what we are hearing.

"Simon Peter answered and said, "You are the Christ, the Son of the living God. Jesus answered and said to him, "Blessed are you, Simon Bar-Jonah, for flesh and blood has not revealed this to you, but My Father who is in heaven." Matthew 16: 17 NKJV

The best revelation you can receive about Jesus is the revelation that comes from God. Some knew Him as a carpenter's son. Others referred to Him as the Prophet. Interestingly, others knew Him as John the Baptist, who happened to be His cousin. However, Peter, had recognized Him by the revelation of God. This is the same revelation that will later bring about a discovery. The revelation we receive from God helps us to know Jesus better.

What revelation have you received from God about Jesus? It is easier to be limited by men's revelation about Jesus based on what they know. Could this be the reason why many people have little or no knowledge about who Jesus is? If you want to have a revelation about Jesus, get to know Him from God.

"When He had been baptized, Jesus came up immediately from the water; and behold, the heavens were opened to Him, and He saw the Spirit of God descending like a dove and alighting upon Him. And suddenly a voice came from heaven, saying, "This is My Beloved Son, in whom I am well pleased.""" Matthew 3: 17 NKJV

From the above scripture, we see that God revealed Jesus as His Beloved son. This gives light to what Jesus referred to about Peter's revelation concerning Him, that *flesh and blood had not revealed it to him, but His Father in Heaven.* Jesus knew that, for men to receive Him as The Anointed Christ, they needed a revelation from God. You can never experience the miraculous power of Jesus without knowing Him as a miracle worker. You can never experience His salvation power without knowing what He gives. Relate with Jesus based on what God reveals Him to be, and it will give discovery to your ministry. Revelation brings discovery. Your discovery will determine the manifestation.

"How God anointed Jesus of Nazareth with the Holy Spirit and with power, who went about doing good and healing all who were oppressed by the devil, for God was with Him." Acts 10: 38 NKJV

"For God so loved the world that He gave His only begotten Son, that whoever believes in Him should not perish but have everlasting life."
John 3: 16 NKJV

"I am the good shepherd. The good shepherd gives His life for the sheep." John 10: 11 NKJV

"While he was still speaking, behold, a bright cloud overshadowed them; and suddenly a voice came out of the cloud, saying, "This is My Beloved Son, in whom I am well pleased. Hear Him!""
Matthew 17: 5 NKJV

CHAPTER THREE

"WHO GOD SAYS YOU ARE."

Living in this world means dealing with challenges, and one of them is what people say about you. Many tend to gossip about others while overlooking their own issues or flaws. If you let your life revolve around others' opinions of you, it becomes crowded with their judgement forgetting that they, like you, also face challenges. Typically, individuals resort to this behavior as an avenue to project their insecurities, problems or frustrations onto others, seeking to improve their own self-esteem. This aligns with the sentiment expressed in Matthew 7:5 by Jesus Christ, highlighting how we often focus on others' faults while neglecting our own, making us hypocrites.

"Hypocrite! First remove the plank from your own eye, and then you will see clearly to remove the

speck from your brother's eye." - Matthew 7:5
NKJV

Simply, put it this way, 'Imagine following the advice of a depressed person?' This should mean that; your life would be impacted by the words of a depressed soul.

"Do people's opinions really matter?"

In as much as it is important to be concerned about what people say about you, you must realize the impact it makes on your life. From this message, we noticed that Jesus was known to be different by the opinion of men; some called him Elijah, others called him John the Baptist, others knew Him as the Prophet Jeremiah. Interestingly, there were some who referred to him as Beelzebub. However, this opinion of men could not determine what God had planned for Him on this earth. Understand, that your progress in life can be hindered by the words of men, and you must therefore approach it with discernment and resilience.

Now when the Pharisees heard it they said, "This fellow does not cast out demons except by Beelzebub, the ruler of demons."- Matthew 12:24 NKJV

Do not be intimidated by the words of men. Focus on what God has said! I would like to share with you, five different accounts indicating God's response to us, as compared to the opinion of men. I pray these accounts would help you discover yourself in Christ.

The woman caught in the act of adultery.
The Opinion of Men
"Then the scribes and Pharisees brought to Him a woman caught in adultery. And when they had set her in the midst, they said to Him, "Teacher, this woman was caught in adultery, in the very act.

Now Moses, in the law, commanded us that such should be stoned. But what do You say?" This they said, testing Him, that they might have something of which to accuse Him. But Jesus stooped down and wrote on the ground with His finger, as though He did not hear." John 8:3-6 NKJV

What God Says You Are
"So when they continued asking Him, He raised Himself up and said to them, "He who is without sin among you, let him throw a stone at her first." And again, He stooped down and wrote on the ground. Then those who heard it, being convicted by their conscience, went out one by one, beginning with the oldest even to the last. And Jesus was left alone, and the woman standing in the midst. When Jesus had raised Himself up and saw only the woman, He said to her, "Woman, where are those accusers of yours? Has no one condemned you?" She said, "No one, Lord." And

Jesus said to her, "Neither do I condemn you; go and sin no more." John 8:7-11 NKJV

Zacchaeus the Tax Collector

The Opinion of Men

But when they saw it, they all complained, saying, "He has gone to be a guest with a man who is a sinner."

Luke 19:7 NKJV

What God Says You Are

"Then Zacchaeus stood and said to the Lord, "Look, Lord, I give half of my goods to the poor; and if I have taken anything from anyone by false accusation, I restore fourfold." And Jesus said to him, "Today salvation has come to this house, because he also is a son of Abraham; for the Son of Man has come to seek and to save that which was lost."" Luke 19:8-10 NKJV

The Prostitute

The Opinion of Men

"Now when the Pharisee who had invited Him saw this, he spoke to himself, saying, "This man, if He were a prophet, would know who and what manner of woman this is who is touching Him, for she is a sinner."
Luke 7:39 NKJV

What God Says You Are

"Then He turned to the woman and said to Simon, "Do you see this woman? I entered your house; you gave Me no water for My feet, but she has washed My feet with her tears and wiped them with the hair of her head. You gave Me no kiss, but this woman has not ceased to kiss My feet since the time I came in. You did not anoint My head with oil, but this woman has anointed My feet with fragrant oil. Therefore, I say to you, her sins, which are many, are forgiven, for she loved much.

But to whom little is forgiven, the same loves little." Then He said to her, "Your sins are forgiven." And those who sat at the table with Him began to say to themselves, "Who is this who even forgives sins?" Then He said to the woman, "Your faith has saved you. Go in peace."" - Luke 7:44-50 NKJV

The Paralytic Man

The Opinion of Men

Then behold, they brought to Him a paralytic lying on a bed. When Jesus saw their faith, He said to the paralytic, "Son, be of good cheer; your sins are forgiven you." And at once some of the scribes said within themselves, "This Man blasphemes!" – Matthew 9:2-3 NKJV

What God Says You Are

"But Jesus, knowing their thoughts, said, "Why do you think evil in your hearts? For which is easier,

to say, 'Your sins are forgiven you,' or to say,
'Arise and walk'? But that you may know that the
Son of Man has power on earth to forgive sins"
then He said to the paralytic, "Arise, take up your
bed, and go to your house.""" Matthew 9:4-6 NKJV

The Leper

The Opinion of Men

"When He had come down from the mountain,
great multitudes followed Him. And behold, a leper
came and worshiped Him, saying, "Lord, if You
are willing, You can make me clean." Matthew
8:1-2 NKJV

What God Says You Are

Then Jesus put out His hand and touched him,
saying, "I am willing; be cleansed." Immediately
his leprosy was cleansed. – Matthew 8:3 NKJV

At one time, the leper felt very low and thought he'd never get better. Sadly, many of you might feel the same, thinking you're not capable of good things because of what happened in the past. Even when God does something amazing, you might doubt if it's really for you. From now on, avoid being limited by the words of people! Hold onto what God says about you. Jesus has forgiven you; you have a fresh start. If you ever feel down, He'll be there for you when you ask. And when you stand up again, He'll be right by your side.

Occasionally, we witness heavy criticism directed at various individuals such as parents, spouses, or religious figures. The information circulated might be true or false. Yet, before we add our voices to the chorus of criticism or condemnation, it's crucial to ponder these essential questions:
How does God view this person?
How does God embrace this person?

What unique qualities or purpose has God bestowed upon this person that people might overlook?

It is important to receive godly revelation, without being quick to judge them. We must focus on how God perceives us, as opposed to men's opinion about us.

Again, I have noticed that the reason why men find something wrong to say about you, is because there is something unique about you that they do not have. I noticed that many people were against Jesus because there was something unique about him, which they didn't have.

"Do you want to continually live your life based on what people say about you?"

Or "Do you want to continually live your life on what God says about you?" If your answer is yes, then, hear the word of the Lord!!

CHAPTER FOUR

"THE REVELATION"

"He said to them, "But who do you say that I am?" Simon Peter answered and said, "You are the Christ, the Son of the living God." Jesus answered and said to him, "Blessed are you, Simon Bar-Jonah, for flesh and blood has not revealed this to you, but My Father who is in heaven. And I also say to you that you are Peter, and on this rock, I will build My church, and the gates of Hades shall not prevail against it. And I will give you the keys of the kingdom of heaven, and whatever you bind on earth will be bound in heaven, and whatever you loose on earth will be loosed in heaven." - Matthew 16:15-19 NKJV

"He said to them, "But who do you say that I am?"

Recognize that Jesus wants you to know Him. Your life as a Christian can never be complete without the Knowledge of Christ. It is very difficult for a property owner to handover his inheritance to a stranger. This is because he lacks familiarity with the stranger. The same way, you must understand that the blessings in Christianity can never manifest without revelation.

"Simon Peter answered and said, "You are the Christ, the Son of the living God."" Matthew 16:16 NKJV

WHO IS JESUS?
Jesus is the Son of the Living God.

"For God so loved the world that He gave His only begotten Son, that whoever believes in Him should not perish but have everlasting life." - John 3:16 NKJV

In today's world, numerous individuals recognize Jesus for the actions attributed to Him rather than understanding His true essence. Many utilize the name of Jesus solely to fulfil their needs without comprehending His significance to them. Peter's perception of Jesus wasn't solely based on His actions but on the revelation of His identity by God. As a Christian, your fullest potential cannot be realized without discovering the essence of Christ by recognizing Him as the Son of the Living God. While some welcome Him for the sustenance He provides, the healings He performs, and the miracles He demonstrates, there remains a crucial necessity for a personal and intimate encounter with Christ. A revelation from God is essential for walking alongside Christ. John 3:16 serves as a confirmation of the identity of the Son of God: God so loved the world. He gave His only begotten Son. That whoever believes in Him should not perish but have everlasting life. It takes the revelation of God's love to reveal who Jesus is, before discovering what He does.

"Blessed are you, Simon Bar-Jonah, for flesh and blood has not revealed this to you, but My Father who is in heaven."

From studying the Bible's history, we learn that anyone who had a divine revelation of God also discovered blessings.

In Genesis 12:1-2, Abram's understanding of God led him to the land promised to his descendants. Later, Abram's name was changed to Abraham, fulfilling God's promise to him. Likewise, in Genesis 28:13, Jacob's encounter with God resulted in a blessing that impacted not only his name, but also his entire lineage.

Now, considering the passages above, Peter's revelation from God brought forth blessings that marked the beginning of a new era. This divine insight was instrumental in shaping a pivotal moment that would alter the course of events, initiating a new dispensation that would impact the world in a profound way. The impact of Peter's revelation throws an insight on how personal encounters help in discovering our purpose in Christ. You need a revelation! Without a revelation, there is no discovery. Without a discovery, there is no manifestation.

As I end, I would like share with you some prayer points that will help you gain access into the room of revelation. You can find it in the next chapter.

CHAPTER FIVE

"PRAYER POINTS"

1. Begin to thank God for the Spirit of Revelation.
2. Oh Lord! As I lift my voice in prayer, Let the Holy Ghost surround my life.
3. Oh God, send your fire to my roots right now. Enter the roots of my life and family, let every wall block my vision break down by fire!
4. As I lift my voice in prayer, any good thing of mine that has been locked in the satanic bank be released right now!
5. Holy Spirit, impact unto me the Spirit of Revelation.
6. Let the anointing of revelation, Come on me now!
7. Every evil ordinance made upon my life shall not prosper! I reverse it!

8. Any farmer planting evil seeds in my life catch fire!

9. Anyone that has vowed that I shall not make it, you shall die in my stead!

10. Every blessing of mine in this season that the enemy is delaying, I declare it be released!

11. Any spell of sleep, cast on me by the devil, break and backfire!

12. Any spell that has made me useless, break and backfire!

13. Any alter that wants to suck my blood, break and scatter by fire!

14. Any alter that hinders people from succeeding or breaking through break and scatter by fire!

15. Any evil eyes looking into my future and destiny, be struck with blindness!

16. My Father and my God, work in me a great deliverance!

17. Thank you, Lord, for an answered prayer in Jesus Name!

AMEN!

Made in the USA
Columbia, SC
15 December 2024

49420364R00020